Mary D. Eldridge Sterling

The Alumnæ Cookbook

Well-tested recipes for table dainties

Mary D. Eldridge Sterling

The Alumnæ Cookbook
Well-tested recipes for table dainties

ISBN/EAN: 9783744781237

Printed in Europe, USA, Canada, Australia, Japan

Cover: Foto ©Lupo / pixelio.de

More available books at **www.hansebooks.com**

—THE—
ALUMNÆ COOKBOOK

WELL-TESTED RECIPES FOR
TABLE DAINTIES

CONTRIBUTED BY

Graduates of the Girls' High and Normal School

PHILADELPHIA

AND SOLD EXCLUSIVELY

FOR THE BENEFIT OF THE TEACHERS' FUND

EDITED BY
MRS. JOHN STERLING
(MARY D. ELDRIDGE)

PHILADELPHIA
BURK & McFETRIDGE, PRINTERS AND PUBLISHERS
306 and 308 Chestnut Street
1891

NOTE

The many kind friends who have rendered assistance, either by contributions or suggestions, in compiling this little book,—especially MRS. HENRY W. HALLIWELL, MISSES JANE AND MARY CAMPBELL, and the CLASS HISTORIANS OF THE ALUMNÆ OF THE GIRLS' HIGH AND NORMAL SCHOOL, PHILADELPHIA,—will accept the editor's sincere thanks. Without their aid so cordially given, we could not have had an ALUMNÆ COOKBOOK.

We may live without poetry, music, and art;
We may live without conscience and live without heart;
We may live without friends; we may live without books;
But civilized man cannot live without cooks

He may live without books,—what is knowledge but grieving?
He may live without hope,—what is hope but deceiving?
He may live without love,—what is passion but pining?
But where is the man that can live without dining?—Owen Meredith

OVERHEARD.

Mr. Public.—I thought that you were already well supplied with cookbooks, my dear.

Mrs. Public.—Oh, so I am; only this, you see, is the "ALUMNÆ" COOKBOOK, and I want it very, very much.

Mr. Public.—And why are you anxious, my dear, to have the "ALUMNÆ" COOKBOOK? So far as I can see, it is simply a bundle of recipes like all the rest of its kind.

Mrs. Public.—[*Aside.*] Now isn't that like a man? [*Aloud.*] Indeed, husband, you are mistaken. Listen one moment, and I will show you wherein lies the difference between the "ALUMNÆ" COOKBOOK and all others. In the first place, not one of its recipes has been put in for "padding,"—in order, merely, to fill out the volume,—and each recipe is vouched for as "good" by its own sender. Again, I find many dear friends among the one hundred contributors. Just fancy! they represent every administration of the Philadelphia Normal School, from '49 to '91— Dr. Wright's, Mr. Cregar's and Mr. Fetter's.

Mr. Public.—Every administration? How interesting!—especially to those who, like ourselves, appreciate the good work that our Normal School has done, and is doing, for this community.

Mrs. Public.—Yes, indeed; not only for this community, though. The daughters who call the Normal School their "Alma Mater" are widely scattered, and each is the centre of some circle of influence wherever she may be. Turning at random the leaves of this little volume, I recognize the names of ladies, one of whom, I know, now lives in California, another in Minnesota, still another in Texas. West, North, South, as well as East have evidently had a share in making the ALUMNÆ COOKBOOK.

Mr. Public.—That reminds me. Wherefore "ALUMNÆ" COOKBOOK?

Mrs. Public.—Just turn to the title-page. See? Every contributor was once a "sweet girl graduate" of the Normal School, and therefore belongs to its "Alumnæ."

Mr. Public.—I understand. [*Reading from title-page.*] "Sold exclusively for the benefit of the Teachers' Fund." Hum! Ha! An excellent purpose. My dear, suppose we take a copy.

Mrs. Public.—Only one?

[*Exeunt Mr. and Mrs. Public soon afterward with several copies of the* ALUMNÆ COOKBOOK, *one for their own use, and the rest to be distributed among friends "for the good of the cause."*]

Alumnae Soups, Fish, and Shellfish

Stop and eat, for well you may
Be in a hungry case.—COWPER.

BLACK BEAN SOUP

BY

MRS. GEO. W. KENDRICK

(Minnie Murdoch)

SOAK over night 1 pint of black beans. In the morning put them on to boil in 2 quarts of cold water. Simmer about 5 hours, adding more cold water as it boils away (about ½ cupful every ½ hour), so there will still be 2 quarts when done. Rub through a strainer, put on to boil again; add 2 teaspoonfuls of salt, 1 saltspoonful each of pepper and mustard, and a pinch of cayenne. As soon as it boils, thicken with 1 tablespoonful of flour and 1 tablespoonful of butter, which have been cooked together. Add more seasoning if required. Slice a lemon and 2 hard-boiled eggs in a tureen, and pour the soup over them.

CLAM SOUP

BY

MRS. WM. J. CLARK

(D. Cornelia Earley)

25 clams, 1 pint of milk, 2 tablespoonfuls butter, 1 heaping tablespoonful flour, 1 teaspoonful minced onion, 1 teaspoonful chopped parsley, a pinch of mace; salt and pepper to taste. Put in a pot the *hard* part of the clams, onion, parsley, mace, and seasoning, with clam liquor increased to

1 quart with water. Cook *covered*, a half-hour after it begins to boil. Heat in another vessel the milk; when hot, stir in the butter rolled in flour and set in a pan of hot water to keep hot after it has boiled two minutes. Strain the soup back into the pot, over the soft part of the clams, the only digestible part, and simmer five minutes. Pour the thickened milk into a *hot* tureen, stir in the soup and serve. (Very good for a flagging appetite.)

CALF'S HEAD SOUP

BY

Miss Kate H. Bunting

Thoroughly clean a calf's head, and boil until meat falls off the bones. Cut the meat in pieces, *not too* small. Tie the brains up in a bag and boil, too. 3 large potatoes cut into pieces about the size of dice, 1 bunch pot-herbs, 1 large onion, the hollow of your hand of cloves, sweet marjoram, summer savory, thyme; rub well and put all in the liquor to boil, about the time the potatoes are put in; pepper and salt to taste. To make the force meat balls get about 1 pound of veal and chop fine. Mix up with sweet marjoram, pepper and salt, and roll into balls about the size of a nickel, dust them with flour and fry brown in butter. Put them on a plate and serve with the soup for those who like them in it. (You may add to the soup after taking from fire a few slices of lemon, and sherry or Madeira wine to taste.) Before taking soup from fire, mix some flour and water together to thicken, but do not get it too thick. We always strain the liquor before putting in the other things so as to get rid of the little bones.

BOILED SHEEPSHEAD

WITH CREAM SAUCE DRESSING

BY

MRS. M. M. GABRYLEWITZ
(Mary M. O'Brien)

Put the fish on to boil in cold water enough to cover it. Do not salt the fish but put salt in the water. Add to the water one carrot sliced, one onion, four cloves, two slices of lemon, three bay leaves, a little parsley, a tablespoonful of vinegar. Let all come slowly to a boil. When the fish is done, take carefully out of water and lay in a flat dish. *For the Dressing:*—Put a tablespoonful of butter in a pan and melt; when melted, add one tablespoonful of flour and mix to a smooth paste. Take from fire and add half a pint of scalded cream and about three tablespoonfuls of the water in which the fish was boiled, to give flavor. Add the yelk of an egg, stir all well together and pour over the fish. To be eaten cold or warm. This sauce can be used for any kind of boiled fish. Hard-boiled egg chopped very fine and parsley spread over the top, may be added if desired.

BAKED SALMON

BY

MISS ELIZABETH McCANDLESS

1 can Hapgood's salmon; 1 cup milk; 1 teaspoonful butter; 2 tablespoonfuls flour; 1 egg. Mix milk, flour, butter together and bring to a boil. Beat egg light. Season the salmon with pepper, salt, and a dust of celery seed. Beat the egg with the salmon and last add the boiling flour, butter, and milk. Stir together and bake half an hour or twenty minutes in a quick oven.

CREAMED OYSTERS

BY

MRS. GEORGE RICHARDS SIKES

(Ellen L. Kenney)

Take fifty large oysters. Stew in their own liquor till the edges curl. Skim out the oysters and put where they will keep warm but not cook. Add to the liquor ½ pint of cream, ½ pint of milk, ¾ cup of butter, salt and pepper to taste. Thicken with 1 dessertspoonful of flour and 2 of cornstarch. Let it boil up and pour over the oysters.

OYSTER CROQUETTES

BY

MRS. BENJAMIN F. BUTCHER

(Lillie R. O'Brien)

Boil 25 oysters five minutes, chop them very fine, add 1 gill of the liquor, 1 gill of cream, 1 tablespoonful of butter and 2 of flour (mixed together), 1 tablespoonful of chopped parsley, 1 tablespoonful of chopped onion, ½ grated nutmeg, salt and cayenne pepper to taste; boil all together until it thickens. When nearly done, add the yelks of 2 eggs, mould, roll in eggs and bread-crumbs, fry in boiling fat.

FRIED OYSTERS

BY

MRS. CHARLES A. MEGUIRE

(Emma E. Geiselman)

Drain large, plump oysters for half an hour through a colander, lifting them with a wooden spoon occasionally to assist in running off the liquor. For each dozen allow three eggs, half a teaspoonful of salt and a pinch of pepper. Mix eggs, pepper and salt thoroughly, and, using your hand, lay the oysters, one at a time, in the egg, then roll in smooth cracker dust, then again in the egg, and, finally, press smooth and shapely in the dust. Spread upon a large tray or biscuit board upon which a little dust has been sifted. Do not pile them on top of each other either now or after frying. When all are prepared heat the lard-bath; it must have a depth of three inches, and be *still* hot before putting in the oysters. Fry not more than four at a time. When a deep golden, take out and lay upon a sheet of soft brown wrapping paper to absorb superfluous grease before transferring to a hot plate. They will puff up, and not only taste, but look the delicious morsels they are, with a crisp, rich crust and juicy, tender hearts.

OYSTER PIE

BY

Mrs. Wm. Stirling

(Rachel N. Thoburn)

75 large oysters; 2 heaping tablespoonfuls of butter; ½ pint of milk; 1 tablespoonful flour; a tiny pinch of ground mace, salt, and a dash of cayenne pepper. For crust, 1 quart sifted flour and a little salt; 1 cup of *sweet* butter; 1 cup of lard; 1 cup of ice water. Have a clear, hot fire. Put the oysters to drain while you make the crust. Put the lard and salt into the flour, cut fine with a sharp knife, and mix as thoroughly as possible. Add the ice water a little at a time, still using the knife until all the flour is wet. Then use the hands as lightly as possible, making it into a ball for your board, which you must dredge lightly. Roll out the dough and baste it with little bits of butter, using the knife, in close rows; dredge a little; turn the ends over, and roll

up as you would a sheet of paper. Roll out, and baste, repeating this until the butter is used up. Line the sides of a pudding dish (about 9 inches diameter) and fill with an inverted cup and bits of stale bread, or, if the bread is not available, a clean napkin. Roll the top out, about an inch thick, cover your mock pie, ornamenting the edge heavily, as this makes it easier to remove. It is now ready for the oven. While it is baking, stew your oysters. Put the milk and the liquor over the fire in separate vessels, rub the butter and flour smooth, skim the liquor as soon as it boils, add the hot milk, the thickening, seasoning, and last the oysters, which should only be allowed to come to a boil, and then drawn away from the fire. In the meanwhile watch your fire and don't let your mock pie burn, as that would spoil the look of it. Time the baking and stewing so as to have them both done at the same time. Remove the pie from the oven to the board, take off the top with a long, broad-bladed knife, take out your mock filling and replace with the oysters, re-cover and send to the table hot. If you have more oysters than the dish will hold, send them to the table in a sauce boat. The pie should bake and the oysters stew in about fifteen minutes.

DEVILED CLAMS

BY

MISS FRANCES M. CARROLL

25 clams cut fine, 5 hard-boiled eggs, 1 large boiled potato, ½ teacup of butter, 1 raw egg, 1 small onion (parboiled), salt, pepper, parsley. Beat potato, butter and yelks together; chop whites and onion. Dip in cracker dust, fry, and place in shells.

LOBSTER CUTLETS

BY

MRS. E. N. GILBERT

(Ellen J. Nolan)

CREAM a piece of butter the size of an egg with flour, and mix in a pint of milk, seasoning with salt, cayenne pepper, finely chopped parsley, and (if desired) a *soupçon* of grated onion. Let the milk come to a boil, stirring constantly, and over the prepared meat of the lobster, coral and white together, pour the sauce, mixing thoroughly. Allow the mixture to cool and stiffen, and then form into cutlets about the size and shape of a large oyster. Roll the cutlets in egg and cracker dust and drop into *boiling* lard. When serving, stick into the corner of each a little claw-tip as garnish. Croquettes of finely minced cold meat can be prepared in the same way.

Alumnae Memorandum Page

Alumnae Memorandum Page

Alumnae Memorandum Page

Alumnae Dishes for Breakfast, Luncheon, or Tea

Pray God, our cheer
May answer my good-will and your good welcome here.—SHAKESPEARE.

Our Way of Cooking Kidney

BY

MRS. ALEXANDER ADAIRE
(Anna M. Soumeillan)

Trim every particle of fat from a fresh beef kidney, and cut the flesh into small pieces. Wash in clear cold water, and drain lightly, then put in a frying pan, cook about five minutes, turning all the time with a fork. Then add a pretty large piece of butter, some pepper and salt to suit the taste. Let this all cook a few minutes and turn out on a hot dish. Serve immediately. Particular care must be taken to add no more water to the kidney than adheres to it after draining.

MEXICAN TAMALES

BY

MRS. THEODORE H. ROE
(Elizabeth W. Dickson)

Boil 2 pounds of veal until tender; salt while boiling. Chop *very* fine, and season with plenty of cayenne pepper and a little garlic. Have ready a thick paste made of 1 cup corn meal mixed with a little boiling water. Shape the veal into rolls the size of the little finger, and encase each in the corn meal paste. Take the inner husks of Indian corn, cut off the ends, leaving the husks about 6 inches long, and wash them in boiling water. Wrap each tamal in corn husk, throw 2 or 3 Mexican peppers into the liquor in which the veal was boiled, and cook the tämälēs in it for 15 minutes. Chicken, with a little fresh pork, can be used instead of veal.

MOINEAUX SANS TÊTE
(Birds without Heads)
BY
MISS CLARISSE E. VALLETTE.

Cut thin slices of *round* steak into pieces about 6 inches square. Chop onion and parsley very fine. Cut bacon into very small dice. Salt and pepper to taste. Put a spoonful of this on each slice of steak. Roll together and tie with thread. Brown these on both sides first, then let simmer on a slow fire for one hour.

CHICKEN TERRAPIN
BY
MRS. LOUIS BRECHEMIN, JR.
(Susan Buckley)

1 chicken, 1 pair sweetbreads, 1 set calves' brains, 1 can mushrooms, ½ cup rich cream, 1 cup sherry, butter the size of an egg, a little nutmeg, pepper and salt to taste. Boil the chicken, not quite so much as for salad, and cut in small pieces, fat, skin, and giblets as well. Boil the brains and sweetbreads in salted water, and the mushrooms until somewhat tender. Cut all in small pieces, add to the chopped chicken, and put all in a saucepan with

enough of the chicken broth to barely cover. Add the cream and the butter rolled in a little flour. Grate a little nutmeg, season with salt and pepper to taste, add half the quantity of sherry and boil until all the ingredients are well mixed and tender. Just before serving add the rest of the sherry and serve boiling hot.

CHICKEN SALAD

BY

MISS MARY MAXWELL

TAKE a pair of large chickens, and, having cleaned and washed them thoroughly, boil until the meat drops from the bones. Skin it and cut into dice. Season with salt and pepper to taste. Cut the white part of three stalks of celery into small pieces. Mix celery and chicken together. *For the Dressing:*—Take the yelks of 3 eggs, 2 tablespoonfuls of olive oil, a *large* tablespoonful mixed mustard. Stir the yelks and mustard together until thick, stir in the oil, and, lastly, add 2 large tablespoonfuls of vinegar, stirring the ingredients together until the mixture is of the consistency of rich cream. Just before serving the salad, add the dressing, and mix well through the chicken and celery.

PRESSED BEEF

BY

MRS. EVELINE FISHER

(Eveline Foster)

3½ pounds finely chopped raw beef. The tender part of the round free from fat and stringy parts is best. Your butcher will grind it for you in the sausage cutter. 6 soda crackers rolled fine. 3 eggs well beaten. 1½ tablespoonfuls of salt. 1 teaspoonful of pepper (scant, if fresh and strong). Mix well together in a loaf. Bake two hours. Eat hot for dinner or cold for tea. Good for picnics.

WELSH RARE-BIT

BY

MISS CECELIA EWING

2 cups of grated cheese, ½ cup milk, yelks of 2 eggs, salt and cayenne to taste. Toast carefully square slices of bread with the crust removed. While hot, butter them, and then plunge in a bowl of hot water. Place them on a heated dish and stand in the oven, while you make the rare-bit. Put the milk into a porcelain-lined or granite saucepan and stand it over a moderate fire. When boiling hot, add the grated cheese; stir continually until the cheese is melted. Add the salt, cayenne, and beaten yelks, and pour it over the toasted bread. A rich cheese must be used or the rare-bit will be tough.

Maccaroni with Cheese

BY

MRS. EMILY S. HARKINS

(Emily S. Bagiot)

½ pound maccaroni, ½ pound Swiss cheese, a penny bunch of parsley and about 6 tablespoonfuls of tomato sauce or roast beef gravy. Break the maccaroni into three or four inches in length and soak in cold water about fifteen minutes. Then boil until tender, in about one-third milk and two-thirds salted boiling water. Drain it well in a colander. Put a layer of maccaroni in the bottom of an earthen dish; add a layer of the cheese grated, sprinkling over it the minced parsley, the tomato sauce or gravy, and a little salt and pepper. Repeat this twice, adding to the top a layer of bread crumbs. Place in the oven and serve when brown.

Fricassee of Potatoes
BY
MRS. M. DILKES CHAUVEAU
(Mary Dilkes)

PLACE a layer of sliced raw potatoes in bottom of baking dish, season with salt, pepper, and bits of butter; then another layer of potatoes and season the same way, and so on until you have the quantity desired. Then cover the whole with milk, place in the oven, and bake until a delicate brown.

POTATO OMELETTE
BY
MRS. JOSEPHINE RITCHIE
(Josephine Johnson)

BOIL 2 large white potatoes, cut them in dice shape, add 2 eggs, ½ small onion chopped fine, 1 pint milk, ¼ pound butter, tablespoonful chopped parsley, pepper and salt. Mix all the ingredients together; through this dredge a little flour. Butter your dish, dredge a little flour on top, and bake brown in a quick oven.

POTATO CROQUETTES
BY
MRS. WM. G. CARROLL
(Elsie M. Beitler)

MIX 2 large cups cold mashed potatoes with 1 tablespoonful melted butter, 1 raw egg, 1 grated onion, 1 tablespoonful cream. Season rather highly with pepper, salt, parsley and sweet marjoram. Form in croquettes, brush with beaten egg, dip in cracker dust, and fry in *hot* lard until a golden brown.

CORN FRITTERS

BY

Mrs. W. A. Garden
(Helen Wyncoop)

1 pint of grated corn, 1 egg, 1 tablespoonful of flour, 3 tablespoonfuls of cream.

Philadelphia Baked Beans

BY

Miss Mary Sterling

Soak over night 3 pints of soup beans in enough water to cover them. Take 1 pound of fresh pork, 2 tablespoonfuls of brown sugar, salt to taste, and add to the beans. Stir all together in an earthen crock, and set to bake in a moderate oven for about three hours. Add a little water from time to time as the beans dry in the baking.

BAKED TOMATOES

BY

Mrs. D. Loughlin
(Kate M. Dornan)

Hollow out centre (half way) of each tomato. Season bread crumbs with pepper, salt, and sweet marjoram, and butter well rubbed through. Fill hollowed-out part of each tomato with the seasoned bread crumbs. Bake in hot oven until thoroughly soft.

TOMATO SALAD

BY

Mrs. Edw. Hewitt

(Mary Stirling)

Two or three hours before meal time peel 5 tomatoes, 1 cucumber, 1 onion, and place them on the ice. Just before the meal is served, slice and arrange on a platter trimmed with lettuce or parsley. Pour over them this dressing:—Mix thoroughly in a bowl 3 tablespoonfuls of oil, 1 teaspoonful of salt, ½ teaspoonful of curry powder, and, last, 1 tablespoonful of vinegar. Suitable for a lunch or tea for four or five people.

CREAM DRESSING

BY

Mrs. Will McCoombs

(Leah Pinto)

This dressing may be used for asparagus, or toast, or dried beef. Put 1 pint of milk in a farina kettle. Beat yelk of 1 egg. Dissolve 1 teaspoonful cornstarch in a little milk, and mix with the yelk. When milk comes to a boil, stir in the mixture; then add a lump of butter, and salt and pepper to taste.

SALTED ALMONDS

BY

Mrs. Horace Subers

(Mary Hay)

Shell, blanch, and spread the almonds on a bright tin pie dish, add a piece of butter the size of a hickory nut, and stand them in a moderate oven until a golden brown. Take them from the oven, stir them around, dredge thickly with salt, and turn them out to cool. *To blanch almonds:*—Shell them, throw them into boiling water, and let them stand on the back part of the range five minutes; then throw them into cold water, and rub them between the hands to remove the skins.

Alumnae Memorandum Page

Alumnae Memorandum Page

Alumnae Pickles and Sauces

All sour things, as vinegar, provoke appetite.—BACON.

CUCUMBER PICKLES

BY

MRS. M. S. ROBERTS

(Margaret S. Rodney)

TAKE 100 small cucumbers and 1 quart of white onions, pare, slice thin, and put in a jar a layer of cucumbers, one of onions and one of salt. Let stand in press all night; then drain off liquor, cover with vinegar, let stand a few hours, and drain dry. Make a mixture of ¼ pound of mustard seed (⅛ pound of it ground and the rest whole), 1 teaspoonful of black pepper, 1 pint of best bottle oil, 1 ounce of celery seed, 2 quarts of vinegar; mix this compound with cucumbers and onions and cover tightly in a jar.

CURRANT SOY

BY

MRS. E. H. AUSTIN

(Clara R. Phillips)

5 pounds of stemmed currants, 3 pounds of brown sugar, 1 pint of cider vinegar, 1 scant tablespoonful of black pepper, 2 scant tablespoonfuls of salt. Put all in a preserving kettle over a moderate fire; cook three hours from the time

the fruit begins to boil. Stir frequently to prevent burning. Keep in glass jars. Excellent with meat.

PICKLED CHERRIES

BY

MRS. EDGAR O. VAN HOUTEN

(E. Allie Blakeley)

SELECT firm cherries. White oxhearts are the best. Remove all specks. *Pack* the cherries in wide-mouthed bottles, or jars. Cover them with vinegar. Pour vinegar off. To each pint of vinegar use from ¾ to 1 pound of granulated sugar. (Quantity of sugar to be determined by strength of vinegar.) Boil vinegar and sugar together from ten to fifteen minutes. Pour over cherries while hot. Into each jar, three or four cloves may be put. Let them stand uncovered till the next day. If any vinegar is left over the jars may be filled as the shrinkage takes place.

PICKLED PEACHES

BY

MRS. S. P. LEE

(Sallie P. Ridgely)

LATE Heath Clings are best both to pickle and to can. Pare and stone the peaches, leaving them *whole*. Stick 3 or 4 cloves in each peach. To 42 peaches take of best white wine vinegar 3 pints, to which add 3 pounds of granulated sugar and 1 ounce of ground cinnamon. Bring this vinegar with its contents (not the peaches) to a boil, and pour, while hot, over the prepared peaches. Let stand for a day or two, then boil the syrup again and pour over the peaches.

Parker House Dressing

BY

Mrs. George D. Cox

(Emma R. Hoopes)

3 eggs; 1 teaspoonful each of salt, mustard, and sugar; 1 cup of oil; ⅔ cup of vinegar; a small quantity of red pepper. Beat the yelks of the eggs with the salt, sugar, pepper and mustard; add the oil slowly, then the vinegar. Beat the whites of the eggs to a stiff froth, adding them last. Put all in a large bowl and set it over a boiling kettle to thicken, stirring it frequently to make it smooth. Remove it from the heat before it becomes too thick. Used for lettuce, cold meats, tomatoes sliced, potato salad, etc. Very useful and handy for housekeepers.

CHILI SAUCE

BY

Mrs. Wm. F. Anderson

(Harriet M. Campbell)

18 large ripe tomatoes, 6 onions, 3 large red or green peppers. Chop all fine, add 3 tablespoonfuls of salt, 5 cups of vinegar. Cook all together one hour.

MRS. P'S COLD CATSUP

BY

Mrs. S. C. Parker

(Sarah Crowe)

1 peck of tomatoes chopped fine, 8 green peppers chopped fine, 4 stalks of horse-radish chopped fine, 1 teacup of yellow mustard seed, 1 teacup of brown sugar, 1 teacup of salt, 2 tablespoons each of ground cloves, allspice, cinnamon; ½

teacup of celery seeds, 1 quart nasturtiums (chopped fine), 3 pints vinegar.

MRS. R'S COLD CATSUP

BY

Mrs. Isaac Remington

(Clemmie W. McCloud)

½ peck ripe tomatoes chopped very fine, 1 small cup salt, 1 small cup black and white mustard seed mixed, 1 cup nasturtiums chopped, 1 small cup of onions chopped, 2 teaspoonfuls black pepper, 2 red peppers chopped without the seeds, 3 stalks of celery chopped, 1 teaspoon each of ground cloves, mace, cinnamon, 1 cupful sugar, 1 quart vinegar. Stir all together. Keep in perfectly air-tight jars.

TOMATO KETCHUP

BY

Mrs Marion A. Bullen

(Marion A. Karcher)

1 peck tomatoes, 1 tablespoon each of red pepper, black pepper, whole cloves, ground allspice, ground mace, ground cinnamon, 2 tablespoons each of mustard seed and celery seed, 4 tablespoons of salt, 1 quart vinegar. Cut up the tomatoes and boil until quite soft. Then strain through a sieve until nothing remains but skin and seeds. To this liquid add the spices, vinegar, etc., and boil until quite thick. Bottle while hot, and if tightly corked will keep for two years without sealing.

Grandma Slifer's Ketchup Sauce

BY

Mrs. Hiram J. Slifer

(Mary Beatty)

1 peck of tomatoes, pared and chopped, 1 teacup of salt, 2 ounces whole black pepper, 1 ounce ground cloves, 2 tablespoons allspice, 2 red peppers, cut fine, 4 large onions. Boil one hour, stirring *all the time*. Just before taking off, add 1 quart strong vinegar. When cold, bottle and seal.

Alumnae Memorandum Page

Alumnae Memorandum Page

Alumnae Memorandum Page

Alumnae Bread, Rolls, and Hot Cakes

> I'm quite ashamed—'tis mighty rude
> To eat so much—but all's so good!—POPE.

HOME-MADE YEAST

BY

MRS. RUSH TAYLOR

(Mary Lingerman)

For one gallon of yeast take 8 large potatoes, 1 cup sugar, 1 cup salt, ½ pint yeast, a handful of hops. Boil the potatoes. When nearly done, add hops (tied in a thin bag), and boil ten minutes longer. Put sugar and salt in an earthen or a porcelain vessel. Lift out hops and press them dry in colander. Mash the potatoes in the water and pass mixture through the colander to the salt and sugar. Add sufficient *boiled* water to make about 3½ quarts. When lukewarm, add yeast. Let stand until perfectly light (about 12 hours). Put in a jug and cork securely. If kept in a cool place this yeast will be good for four or five weeks.

HOME-MADE BREAD

BY

MRS. NORRIS H. NORDEN

(Helen E. Freas)

For one small loaf of bread take 1 quart sifted flour, ½ pint of milk, 1 tablespoonful of butter, 1 teaspoonful of sugar, ½ teaspoonful of salt. *To set the sponge:*—The flour is sifted carefully and into the centre is poured the yeast (½ cake), which has been previously mixed with a little water added to the half pint of lukewarm milk. Beat the sponge well and set to rise. When it becomes light, add sugar, butter and salt. Knead well and set to rise again. Bake in a moderate oven.

Nonpareil Corn Bread

BY

MRS. GEORGE CROSBY

(Ella Fagen)

2 heaping cups of Indian meal, 1 cup flour, 2 eggs, 2½ cups of milk, 1 teaspoonful lard, 2 teaspoonfuls white sugar, 1 teaspoonful soda, 2 teaspoonfuls cream-tartar, 1 teaspoonful salt. Beat the whites and yelks of the eggs separately and thoroughly; then melt the lard and add. Into the dry meal and flour mixed, sift the soda and cream-tartar, and add these to the eggs, lard, and milk. Beat vigorously. Bake in a quick and steady oven for thirty minutes.

SALLY LUNN

BY

MRS. JOHN COBB

(Sarah A. Redles)

¼ pound of butter (melted); 4 eggs, yelks and whites beaten separately; 1 pint of milk; ½ teaspoonful of salt; about 4 teaspoonfuls of Royal Baking Powder; enough flour to make a stiff batter. Bake about half an hour in a quick oven.

HOT BISCUIT

BY

Mrs. M. C. Geisler

(Mary C. Dickes)

1 pint hot milk poured over ⅓ cup lard; add, when nearly cool, ½ cup yeast, ½ teaspoonful salt, flour to make a thick sponge. Let it stand until light (about three hours) and then knead, adding 1 tablespoonful sugar, and flour if necessary. After a second rising roll out and cut into biscuits about a half hour before baking. Bake twenty minutes in a hot oven.

POP OVERS

BY

Mrs. John R. Angney

(Martha P. Hand)

2 eggs, 2 cups of flour, 2 cups of milk, 1 teaspoonful of baking powder. Mix flour and milk; add the eggs, beating yelks and whites separately; add baking powder just before placing in the oven. Butter deep gem pans or cups and place in the bottom of the oven. When nearly done put in the top part of the oven until brown. To be eaten with custard or cornstarch made thin, using eggs.

GRAHAM GEMS

BY

Mrs. Chas. G. Saul

(Lidie Bower)

1 quart milk, 1 quart flour, (half Graham), 2 eggs, 1 pinch of salt. Have pans hot and bake thirty minutes.

MUFFINS

BY

MRS. MAURICE F. EGAN

(Kate C. Mullin)

1 cup of milk, 2 eggs (the yelks to be beaten with the milk, the whites to a stiff froth), 1 tablespoonful melted butter, 2 teaspoonfuls Royal Baking Powder, a little salt, flour to make like cake. Bake in well-greased rings or gem pans.

MILTON MUFFINS

BY

MISS MARY A. CAMPBELL

One egg, 1 pint of milk, 1 pint of flour, a pinch of salt. Beat one egg very light, add part of the milk, all of the flour, then add the rest of the milk. Bake twenty minutes in buttered tins. Eat hot.

BATTER CAKES

BY

MRS. S. H. R. CAPEN

(Sarah H. Reger)

To one cup of thick cream add enough flour to make a stiff batter. Beat thoroughly. Add the beaten yelks of two eggs and a teaspoonful of bi-carb. soda. Mix well, salting slightly. Toss in the beaten whites of the two eggs and bake on a griddle.

# Alumnae Memorandum Page

Alumnae Memorandum Page

Alumnae Puddings and Pastry

More than enough for nature's ends,
With something left to treat my friends.—MALLET.

CHERRY PUDDING

BY

MRS. CHAS. M. LUKENS

(Matilda C. Barns)

For a family of five persons, boil 4 potatoes (pared) with salt in the water. When done, drain and mash them quickly, and, while still hot, stir in enough flour to roll out. On this sprinkle your seeded cherries (morellas are best), sprinkle with sugar, roll neatly up, put into a cloth or a pudding bag (not too small) and boil or steam for 4 hours. If the water evaporates fill up with boiling water. Eat with butter and sugar (hard sauce) into which is stirred the white of 1 egg and 1 tablespoonful of brandy. A dyspeptic may eat this crust with impunity. The same crust will do for dumplings.

BLACKBERRY MUSH

BY

MISS MARY J. CAIRL

1 quart of blackberries, 1 pint water, 1 tablespoonful cornstarch. Stew the blackberries in water until well done, add sugar to taste, thicken with cornstarch dissolved in a little cold water. Boil a few minutes after adding cornstarch. When cool, flavor with vanilla. To be eaten cold with cream.

PLUM PUDDING

BY

Mrs. Walter R. Livingston

(Elizabeth A. Ziegler)

1½ cups of bread crumbs, 1½ cups of flour, 1½ cups of sugar, ½ teaspoonful of salt, 3 eggs and ½ cup of milk, 1 teaspoonful each of cinnamon and nutmeg, ½ pound of beef suet chopped fine, ½ pound each of raisins and currants, ¼ pound of citron. Mix the bread crumbs, sugar, suet, and fruit thoroughly; add the eggs and milk. Sift in the flour, add the salt, and put the spices in last. Pour in a greased mould and steam three hours. To be eaten with hard sauce.

PAPA'S PUDDING

BY

Mrs. W. H. List

(Ella Murdoch)

1 cup of molasses, 1 cup of beef suet, 1 cup of milk, 1 cup of raisins, 1 cup of currants, 2 heaping teaspoonfuls of baking powder, enough flour to make a batter stiff enough to drop. Put into a bag, allowing sufficient room to swell, and boil 3 hours. Make a sauce to eat with it, according to taste. We use beaten butter and sugar flavored with vanilla.

MARYLAND PUDDING

BY

Mrs. A. J. Hurlock

(Annie J. Tomkins)

3 coffee cups of flour, 1 teaspoonful of soda, 2 teaspoonfuls cream of tartar. Sift into pan together with ½ teaspoonful of salt. Make a well in the centre of flour, into which drop yelks of 4 eggs. Stir, gradually adding 1½

pints of milk. Last of all, add the well-beaten whites. Bake 1 hour in a moderately hot oven. Eaten with sauce, either sweetened cream flavored with vanilla, or Nun's butter.

Indian Pudding—The "Champion"

BY

Mrs. M. A. Ely

(Marian Ash)

Into 1 quart of *boiling* milk stir 1 cup of fine Indian meal, and let stand until lukewarm. Mix with this batter 1 level teaspoon of salt, 2 ounces of melted butter, ¼ pound of sugar, the same of raisins (floured), and 4 eggs well beaten. Stir thoroughly and bake 1½ hours. Eat with cream, or hard sauce.

Boiled Fruit Pudding

BY

Mrs. Annie C. Dorland

(Annie Caley)

1 pint of flour, 1 heaping teaspoonful of baking powder, salt to taste, and butter the size of an egg. Sift the baking powder well through the flour, rub the butter thoroughly into this, and use cold milk enough to make a light dough. Roll this into a square about an inch thick, and spread it with fruit, leaving a margin of an inch all around. Wet the edges slightly, roll up and sew in a cloth which has been wrung out of hot water and well dredged with flour. Boil or steam one hour, and serve with cream and sugar, or hard sauce.

RICE PUDDING

BY

MRS. FRANK A. MULLIKEN

(Annie Housekeeper)

3 ounces rice, 2 quarts milk, sugar to taste, a pinch of salt, nutmeg to taste. Bake in a slow oven two hours, or until the rice is thoroughly cooked, and the milk is of the consistency of rich cream.

An Excellent Rice Pudding

BY

MRS. D. F. SAYRE

(Lydia F. Hamor)

PUT 6 tablespoons of rice in an earthen basin. Soak for an hour in barely enough cold water to cover it. Add 2 quarts of milk (Alderney is best) and a tablespoon of Vanilla Extract. Sweeten to taste, and bake three hours in a moderate oven. When *done*, the milk will be very deep yellow and of the consistency of thick cream. Keep stirring from the bottom about every twenty minutes until nearly done; then let it brown. After cooling, put in the refrigerator.

A Palatable Dessert

BY

MISS MAUDE M. JENKINS

Mix well together the juice and grated rind of 1 lemon, 1 cup of sugar, 1 piece of butter the size of an egg, 2 eggs, 1 tablespoonful cornstarch, and 1½ cups boiling water. Boil until the mixture thickens. While still warm, pour over sliced cake or lady fingers, and then allow to cool.

CHOCOLATE CUSTARD

BY

MRS. S. W. DUNGAN
(Sarah A. Walker)

1 quart milk, 6 eggs, 2 ounces sugar, 2 ounces chocolate, 1 tablespoonful of rose water. Chip the chocolate and add sufficient boiling water to make it smooth. Mix with it, gradually, the boiling milk. When cool enough, stir in it the beaten eggs, sugar, and rose water. Bake in a moderately hot oven. Serve hot.

FRENCH CUSTARD

BY

MISS CORNELIA W. ELMES

1 quart milk, 4 eggs, 1 tablespoonful sugar, 1 tablespoonful cornstarch, 1 teaspoonful vanilla. Put the milk on to boil in a farina boiler. Beat the yelks with the sugar and cornstarch, then add them to the boiling milk. Then put the custard into the pudding dish. Make a meringue of the beaten whites of the eggs with 1 tablespoonful of pulverized sugar and a teaspoonful of vanilla. Drop the meringue over the custard, and place it in the oven only long enough to brown the meringue.

SNOW PUDDING

BY

MRS. WALTER T. LEE
(Nellie I. Morris)

1 pint of milk, 2 tablespoons of cornstarch, 3 eggs, ½ cup sugar. Dissolve the cornstarch in a little of the milk and the sugar in the remainder. When it begins to boil add the dissolved cornstarch, stirring constantly

until it becomes a smooth paste. Then remove from fire and add the whites of eggs, beaten to a stiff froth. Pour into individual moulds and serve with a custard made of the yelks of the eggs, 1 pint of milk, sugar and flavoring to taste.

CABINET PUDDING

BY

MISS KATE S. GILLESPIE

1 dozen almonds blanched and pounded, ½ dozen English walnuts and ½ dozen black walnuts cut or broken into particles, small piece of citron cut very fine, 1 even cupful of raisins boiled till tender and seeded. Mix well these ingredients in a bowl and prepare the following pudding: Take 1 quart of milk, leaving out enough to wet 3½ tablespoonfuls cornstarch. Bring the milk to the boil, add the cornstarch into which have been beaten the yelks of 2 or 3 eggs, as preferred, and 4 tablespoonfuls sugar. When the cornstarch is thoroughly cooked, take from the fire, flavor with lemon extract, and stir in the nuts, citron, and raisins. Then pour into cups, adding a macaroon to each cup. When cold turn out of the cups and serve with the following sauce: Beat the yelk of an egg and 1½ tablespoonfuls sugar together, add a large cupful cream and a teaspoonful vanilla. If the cream is too rich, part milk may be used. The white of an egg beaten very light, added, is an improvement.

Delicious Hazelnut Tart

BY

MRS. A. B. AUSBACHER

(Frances Eger)

Open 1 pound of hazelnuts; grate them fine, or chop them in an almond grater. Take yelks of 10 eggs, beat them very light, add 12 ounces powdered sugar. Beat again till quite thick. Add 1 teaspoonful of rose water or one of vanilla flavoring. Then, froth very stiff the whites of 10 eggs and stir the froth into the eggs and sugar, adding very lightly, a little at a time, 6 ounces of flour (sifted twice) and ⅓ of the grated hazelnuts. Bake in two pans so as to have two layers. When baked and quite cold, you place between the two layers a mixture composed of the rest of the grated nuts, which have been stirred into one pint of *thick whipped* sweet cream flavored with a pinch of dry vanilla bean.

CHEESE CAKE PIE

BY

MRS. GEO. H. STOUT

(Frances A. Widdifield)

To five cents' worth of cottage cheese add ½ tablespoonful of butter, ½ tablespoonful flour, juice and rind of ½ lemon, 3 eggs (yelks and whites beaten separately), 1 tablespoonful cream; sweeten to the taste and add a pinch of salt. Dust a little ground cinnamon on top just before putting into the oven. This quantity makes one *large* pie. Use one crust only.

CHEESE CUSTARD PIE

BY

MRS. DAVID W. HUNT

(Josephine Dunlap)

1 quart dry cottage cheese, 2 ounces butter, 1 pound sifted sugar, 2 eggs, 1 tablespoon flour, ½ nutmeg (grated), pinch of salt, rind and juice of 1 lemon. Dress the curd very smooth with a wooden spoon. Beat the butter and half of sugar to a cream. Then add remaining sugar, cheese, flour, salt, and flavoring. Beat eggs light and stir in just before baking. Bake in crust. This will make two pies.

MOCK MINCE PIE

BY

MRS. CHARLES HARTE

(Kate Kereven)

1 cup each of stoned raisins and of washed currants, ½ cup of cut citron, 1 cup each of brown sugar, of molasses, of cider, 2 cups of apples pared, cored, and chopped fine, 1 lemon (juice and grated rind), 3 Boston (or 4 soda) crackers rolled fine, 2 tablespoonfuls of vinegar, ½ teaspoonful of ground cinnamon, ½ teaspoonful of ground allspice, ¼ teaspoonful of cloves, ¼ teaspoonful of mace. Mix the ingredients thoroughly, and if the mixture should not be moist enough, add cider (or water) to moisten it. Line two deep pie plates with good plain paste, fill them with the mixture, and put on an upper crust; then bake the pies thirty minutes in a quick oven.

Temperance Mince-Meat

BY

Mrs. George E. Sladen

(Eliza A. Fischer)

2 pounds lean beef, ¾ pound of beef suet, 1 heaping tablespoonful ground cloves, ½ nutmeg (grated), ¼ pound candied lemon peel, ¼ pound citron, 1 pound small seedless raisins, 1 pound currants (cleaned and dried). Boil the beef till very tender, set it away for a day or more to be perfectly dry and cold, then chop it so fine that it becomes mealy when rubbed in the hands. Remove from the suet all stringy substances, chop it fine and mix with the meat. Now add all the other ingredients. This dry mixture will keep all winter in an air-tight jar. When ready to make pies, add chopped apples and sugar to taste, and for moistening take equal parts of New Orleans molasses and best cider vinegar (diluted with water and a little sugar).

Alumnae Memorandum Page

Alumnae Memorandum Page

Alumnae Memorandum Page

Alumnae Ices and Sweets

I always thought cold victual nice:—
My *choice* would be vanilla-ice.—O. W. HOLMES.

FROZEN CUSTARD

BY

MRS. HENRY W. HALLIWELL

(Lizzie Settle)

TAKE 3 pints of cream, 1 quart of milk, 12 eggs, 2½ coffee cups sugar, 1 small vanilla bean. Cut the bean in several pieces, scrape out the seeds in a gill of milk and gently boil seeds and bean, to extract full flavor. Scald, in a preserving or custard kettle, the cream and milk, but do not boil it. Beat the eggs until light, adding the sugar until all is thick and smooth. Stir slowly the cream and milk into the beaten egg and sugar, add the boiled bean and milk and replace on the fire. *Stir constantly* until it becomes of the consistency of thin custard. Remove from the fire at once, and strain through a wire sieve into the ice cream freezer, which latter set in a pail of cold water. When cool, freeze as ice-cream.

Frozen Strawberries

BY

MRS. ANNA W. MCKINLEY

(Anna R. Winchester)

COVER 1 pound of berries with 1 pound of sugar. When the sugar is melted, mash the berries, add 1 pint of water and freeze.

Frozen Charlotte Russe

BY

Mrs. William Bickley

(Lucy R. McElroy)

½ package of gelatine dissolved in ½ pint cold water. 3 eggs, 1 pint new milk, boiled to a custard. Pour on gelatine, add 1 pound sugar, and strain. When cold, add ½ pint brandy and 1 tablespoonful vanilla. When it begins to set in the freezer, stir in 3 pints of whipped cream.

ORANGE MERINGUE

BY

Mrs. F. C. McCurdy

(Florence A. Cathcart)

Soak ½ box gelatine in a pint of cold water for a half hour, bring to the boiling point and carefully stir in the well beaten yelks of 3 eggs mixed with a cup of sugar. Take from the fire and flavor with the juice of 1 lemon and 2 or 3 oranges according to size. Let it stand on the ice till cold and stiff. Turn into a glass dish and heap up over it the whites of 3 eggs beaten until stiff with 3 tablespoonfuls of powdered sugar gradually sifted in.

FRUIT GELATINE

BY

Mrs. Edward Zieber

(Margaret Jean MacVeagh)

1 box Cox's gelatine, 6 oranges, 3 lemons (more will be needed if the fruit is small), 1 pound granulated sugar, 3 bananas. Pour 1 pint of cold water over the gelatine, and let it dissolve. Mix 1 pound of sugar with the juice of

4 oranges and 3 lemons, and the grated rind of 1 orange and 2 lemons. Pour one pint of *boiling* water over the partly-dissolved gelatine, and add the other ingredients. Mix thoroughly and strain. Pour into moulds or dishes. Slice the bananas and remaining oranges over it, and set in the refrigerator until it becomes solid. If the weather is warm, it will harden better in tin than in earthenware.

FRENCH TAPIOCA

BY

Mrs. Edward Fiss

(Mary C. Morris)

5 scant tablespoonfuls flake tapioca, 1 quart milk, 1 pint water, 1 *small* cupful sugar, 3 eggs, whites and yelks beaten separately, 2 teaspoonfuls vanilla. Soak the tapioca in the water over night, or for five hours, in a cool place. Heat the milk to boiling, in a vessel set within another of boiling water, add the tapioca and water in which it was soaked, and a pinch of salt, stirring occasionally. When all is boiling hot, add the yelks of the eggs, beaten very light, with the sugar, and stir until it thickens perceptibly, but do not let it boil too long or the custard will break. Remove from fire and stir in briskly, but carefully, the whites of eggs beaten to a stiff froth, and the vanilla. When sufficiently cool, pour into a glass dish and set away to get very cold.

Mrs. L's Lemon Butter

BY

Mrs. L. J. Logan
(E. Terese Dickes)

Juice and rind of 2 lemons, 2 eggs well beaten, 1½ teacups of sugar, 2 tablespoonfuls of butter. Beat eggs and sugar together, add butter and lemons. Boil five minutes, stirring all the time.

Mrs. M's Lemon Butter

BY

Mrs. Emma J. Morris
(Emma J. Fort)

Take the juice and grated rinds of 4 lemons, 5 eggs, 2½ tumblers of sugar, 1 tumbler of butter. Beat well together and boil five minutes.

Fruit Candy

BY

Miss E. S. Tait

4 cups of granulated sugar, 1 cup of water, 1 cup of vinegar, butter the size of a walnut. Boil until it hardens in cold water. Pour it into buttered tins, in which have been placed nuts, dates, figs, etc.

Alumnae Taffy

BY

Miss Sara Hawks Sterling

1 pound of brown sugar, 1 scant cup of water, butter the size of an egg, 1 teaspoonful ground ginger. Put sugar and water in a saucepan, and when the mixture comes to a boil add the melted butter and

ginger. Boil without stirring until the taffy hardens quickly in cold water. Remove from fire and place in buttered tins to cool. Vanilla, or other flavoring, may be used instead of ginger, and nuts may be added, if desired.

Alumnae Memorandum Page

Alumnae Memorandum Page

Alumnae Memorandum Page

Alumnae Cakes

Dainty bits
Make rich the ribs.—SHAKESPEARE.

Moravian Christmas Cookies

BY

MRS. WM. J. LAMBERTON

(Mary McCurdy)

1 pound brown sugar, 1 pound butter, 4 pounds flour, 1 quart New Orleans cooking molasses, ½ ounce ginger, ½ ounce cloves, 1 ounce cinnamon, 1 teaspoon soda, juice of one large orange. Mix all together, except the flour, being careful to heat enough to melt the butter. Then "work in" the flour. This makes a large quantity, as the cakes should be rolled very thin. Keep the cookies in a dry place, and they will be crisp and delicious as long as they last, even for months.

SUGAR BISCUIT

BY

MRS. A. R. THOMAS

(Evelyn S. Rigler)

1 pint of milk, 1 pound of flour, 1½ cups of sugar, 1 egg, 2 ounces of lard, ½ teaspoonful of salt, 1 teacup of yeast or ½ yeast cake; flavor with a little nutmeg, cinnamon, lemon or orange. Boil the milk; when it is lukewarm, dissolve in it half a yeast cake. Measure in your pan 1 pound of flour; add *1 cup* of sugar, 1 egg, 2 ounces of lard, the salt and the flavor. Mix these ingredients with the milk in which

the yeast has been dissolved, and stir until the lumps are all gone. After mixing thoroughly beat steadily for five minutes, sprinkle a little flour over the top and set to rise. Cover the sponge so it will be warm. (When yeast is used, mix with the milk and add the yeast last, beating thoroughly.) In the morning, add to the light sponge the other ½ *cup* of sugar and make into a soft dough. (Be careful not to make the dough stiff.) Let this rise again, and when light mold into small biscuits. Set these to rise, letting them get quite light before baking. When risen enough, bake in a hot oven until done (about thirty minutes).

DOUGHNUTS

BY

MRS. CHARLES B. STRETCH

(Anna Humphrey)

1 pint milk, ½ pound shortening (half butter, half lard), yeast cake, enough flour to make it stiff. When light, add 1 pound sugar, 3 eggs, ½ nutmeg, and mold into a loaf. When again light, roll out and cut and boil, dipping each one in a mixture of cinnamon and sugar as it is taken from the boiling lard.

SOFT GINGERBREAD

BY

MRS. J. B. BRENNISER

(Lizzie S. Cuskaden)

1 cup sugar, 1 cup shortening—half butter and half lard, 1 cup New Orleans molasses, 1 cup milk, 2 eggs, 1 teaspoonful ginger, 1 teaspoonful cinnamon, 1 teaspoonful soda dissolved in warm water. Flour, sufficient to make a drop dough. Bake in muffin pans.

BUTTER CAKES

BY

Mrs. A. H. Marcus

(Sophie Marcus)

Put into a large dish 1 pound of the best butter, 1 pound of granulated sugar, 2 pounds flour well sifted, the grated rind of 2 lemons, 1 teaspoonful of vanilla extract, 3 eggs well beaten, 2 tablespoonfuls of milk, 2 teaspoonfuls of baking powder. Work with the hands until it comes together, roll very thin, cut, sprinkle a little granulated sugar on each cake, and bake in a hot oven.

SCOTCH CAKES

BY

Mrs. Howard S. Stetler

(Ida Dwier)

1 pound flour, 1 pound sugar, ¾ pound butter, 3 eggs, 1 teaspoonful cinnamon and cloves. Roll out very thin in equal quantities of sugar and flour. Half the quantities may be used with good result.

Shellbark Macaroons

BY

Mrs. Leon Gans

(Teresa Hamburger)

Beat the whites of 3 eggs stiff and add ½ pound pulverized sugar, and, last, ½ pound shellbark kernels that have been reduced to a flour by enclosing in a bag, putting on board, and pounding with potato masher. Drop the mixture from teaspoon on greased pan—be sure to allow a good space between—and bake till yellow brown. After taking from oven, allow to set about one minute. (We consider these very fine.)

YORK STATE SNAPS

BY

MRS. FRANKLIN COLLIER

(Emma Kauffman)

1 cup of dark sugar (hard to get), 1 cup of New Orleans molasses, ½ cup of shortening of any kind, 1 teaspoonful ground cinnamon, ½ teaspoonful ground cloves, ¼ teaspoonful soda dissolved in a little water, enough flour to roll very thin. Bake in a quick oven. Place in an earthen jar. Housekeepers will find that *they will not keep*, unless under lock and key.

Old-Fashioned Dutch Cake

BY

MRS. WM. MCCAMBRIDGE

(Laura G. Fagen)

For the sponge take 1 quart and 1 pint of flour, 1 quart of warm water, 1 tablespoonful sugar, 1 tablespoonful lard, 1 cent's worth baker's yeast. Melt the lard and sugar in the warm water. Stir this into the flour, which must be sifted. Lastly, stir in the yeast. Beat up hard for several minutes and set to rise over night. The next morning sift 2 quarts and 1 pint of flour in a deep bread tray with 2 tablespoonfuls of salt. Into this mix thoroughly ½ pound roll butter and ¼ pound lard. Make a hole in the middle of the heap, into which put the following:—1 nutmeg grated, 3 cups sugar, 2 eggs, ½ pound sultana raisins and ¼ pound currants—washed and dried, the risen sponge. Work this the same as bread. Then divide into loaves, putting these into well-greased, round, deep pans. Set the pans in a warm place (over the range, if possible), with a cloth thrown over them to exclude the air and dust. Let rise from five to six hours. Then bake in a moderate oven one hour, or until a clean straw, run through the thickest part, will come out clean.

HARTFORD TEA CAKE

BY

Miss Mattie A. Cairl.

7 cups of flour, 6 cups of sugar, 3 cups of butter, 3 cups of milk, 8 eggs, ½ glass of brandy warmed in milk, 2 pounds of raisins, 2 pounds of currants, 1½ pounds of citron, spices to taste, 4 teaspoonfuls of baking powder sifted through the flour. Cream the butter and sugar; add the beaten yelks, milk, and spices. Then, the whipped whites stirred in alternately with the flour. Lastly, the fruit.

LONG ISLAND CAKE

BY

Mrs. Charles Burr

(Henrietta Thomas)

½ pound butter, 1 pound sugar, 1 pound flour, 4 eggs, ½ pint milk, baking powder. Add fruit—raisins, currants, and citron. This will keep for some time.

STOCK GRANGE CAKE

BY

MISS JANE CAMPBELL

1 pint of milk, 1 pound of sugar, 1 pound of flour, ½ pound of currants, ¼ pound of butter, 1 nutmeg, cinnamon to taste, 3 even teaspoons baking powder. Bake in a medium oven.

FRUIT CAKE

BY

MRS. S. S. CAVIN

(M. A. Mecaskey)

1 pound of butter, 1 pound of flour, 1 pound of sugar, 10 eggs, 1 tablespoonful of vanilla, 2 teaspoonfuls of ground cinnamon, ½ teaspoonful of ground cloves, ½ cup cream or milk, 1½ pounds of raisins (seeded and chopped), 1½ pounds currants (washed, picked, and dried), ¾ pound of citron (washed, wiped dry, and cut in small, thin pieces), ½ cup cold coffee. Beat the butter and sugar to a cream. Whisk the eggs until thick, and add them by degrees with the spices and vanilla. Then stir in cream and one-fourth the flour. Add the coffee, and the remainder of the flour, half at a time. Lastly, add the fruit, and beat all well together. Butter your pan and line with white paper; put in the mixture, spread it smooth over the top with a knife, and bake in a moderate oven about four hours.

WASHINGTON CAKE

BY

Mrs. George W. Elkins

(Frances L. Standbridge)

3 ounces butter, 6 ounces sugar, 7 ounces flour, 2 eggs well beaten, 1 gill of sour milk or buttermilk, pinch of mace, 1 tablespoonful vinegar, ¼ of level teaspoonful of baking soda dissolved in a little sweet milk. Cream butter and sugar together, add the well-beaten eggs and the sour milk, then flour (sifted), mace, vinegar and soda. Bake in a *moderate* oven.

SOFT ICING CAKE

BY

Mrs. J. K. Barton

(Millie S. Scott)

Boil 6 ounces of granulated sugar and 3½ tablespoonfuls of water together for eight or ten minutes. Beat the yelks of four eggs very light; save out the white of one for the icing; beat the remaining whites to a stiff froth. Pour the boiling water and sugar over the beaten yelks and beat until cold. Sift ¼ pound of flour, and stir in alternately the whites and the flour. Flavor with a tablespoonful of extract of vanilla. Bake in a well-greased pan about twenty minutes (a square pan cuts better slices). *Icing:*—1 tea cup granulated sugar and 3 tablespoonfuls of water; boil together about ten minutes. Beat the remaining white very stiff, pour the boiling water and sugar into it, beat until cold, and spread over top and sides of cake.

A DELICATE CAKE

BY

MRS. WILLIAM STOUT

(Ellen T. Jones)

TIME: About 1 hour. Articles: 1 pound of sugar, 1 pound of flour, 7 ounces of butter, whites of 6 eggs, ½ nutmeg grated, a little lemon extract. *Directions:*—Beat the butter to a cream and stir into it the sugar and flour, then add the whites of eggs beaten to a froth, the grated nutmeg, and the lemon extract. Beat all well together and put into a tin lined with buttered paper. 5 or 6 ounces of powdered almonds may be added to this cake, according to your taste.

SPONGE CAKE

BY

MRS. JAMES HARTE

(Emma Coulomb)

1 cup sifted flour, 4 eggs, 1 cup of sugar (A), 1 tablespoonful of vinegar, flavor to taste. Beat the eggs and sugar together for twenty minutes. Add (without beating) the flour. Flavor, and stir in the vinegar as gently as possible. Bake in a moderate oven about half an hour. Butter the pan and bake immediately.

BOILED SPONGE CAKE

BY

MISS ELLA S. BRADEN

YELKS of 7 eggs; whites of 6 eggs; ¾ pound granulated sugar and 6 tablespoonfuls water boiled until clear; pour slowly over the beaten whites and yelks, stirring while pouring. When cool, add

½ pound sifted flour (stir, not beat). Flavor to taste. Bake in a long pan twenty-five or thirty minutes in a very slow oven.

SPONGE GINGER CAKE

BY

Mrs. George Clement
(Margaret Macaulay)

2 cups sugar, 1 cup molasses, 1 cup butter, 4 eggs, 1 cup sour milk, 3 cups flour, ½ teaspoonful soda, 2 teaspoonfuls ginger.

ALMOND CREAM CAKE

BY

Mrs. Wm. T. Burke
(Florence T. Kennedy)

2 cups sugar, ½ cup butter, 1 lemon—juice and grated rind, 4 eggs—3 whites and 4 yelks beaten separately, 1 cup cold water, 3 cups flour, 3 even teaspoonfuls baking powder.

Cream the butter and sugar, add the lemon, the yelks, the water, the flour and powder sifted together, and the whites. Beat hard and bake in jelly cake tins. *Filling:*—1 cup milk, 3 even teaspoonfuls cornstarch, yelk of 1 egg, ½ cup sugar, ½ cup almonds, blanched and chopped fine, 1 teaspoonful vanilla. Heat the milk to boiling, thicken with cornstarch wet in a little cold milk, pour in the whipped yelks and sugar, and cook all ten minutes, stirring constantly. Then cool, add flavoring and almonds. *Icing:*—Whip the two reserved whites to a stiff froth, add a few drops lemon juice, and sufficient pulverized sugar to make thick enough to spread. Cover top and sides. Before it hardens lay the kernels of English walnuts in two layers or circles on top of cake.

EDGE HILL CAKE

BY

Miss Ella P. Macaulay

2 cups granulated sugar, ½ cup butter, 4 eggs, ½ cup milk, 2 cups flour, 2 teaspoonfuls baking powder. Cream butter and sugar; then add beaten yelks of eggs; next the milk. Mix baking powder and flour thoroughly together, and add flour and well-beaten whites of eggs alternately. Flavor with 1 teaspoonful vanilla, and bake in three layer pans. *Icing:*—Whites of 2 eggs well beaten, 1 cup pulverized sugar, ½ cup water. Boil sugar and water until the mixture hairs or strings from the spoon. When cool, add whites of eggs and flavor with vanilla.

LAYER SPONGE CAKE

BY

Mrs. Wm. C. Crowell

(Jennie Macauley)

5 eggs, 2 cups granulated sugar, 2 cups flour (sifted), 1 teaspoonful Royal Baking Powder, ½ cup boiling water, flavor to taste (rose water preferred). *Directions:*—Beat the yelks and whites of eggs separately (reserving the white of one egg for icing); then add the sugar to the yelks; then, whites of eggs; next, flour and baking powder; lastly, put in boiling water and place immediately in oven. Bake in two layers, and when cold ice with following icing: 1 cup granulated sugar, 4 tablespoonfuls water; boil together seven minutes; then pour into the white of the egg, which has been well beaten. Beat all the time you are pouring the sugar into the egg; flavor; then spread on cakes when both are cool.

SPICE CAKE

BY

Mrs. Isaiah Rudy
(Laura Dales)

½ cup butter, 2 cups sugar, 3 eggs (leave out the whites of 2 of them), 1 cup sour milk, 1 teaspoonful baking soda (or, you can use sweet milk with 2 teaspoons baking powder), flour enough for rather a stiff dough, 1 heaping spoon of ground cinnamon. Dissolve the soda in a little boiling water, put in last. Bake in three layers. Ice in between the layers, thickly, using for this the two whites you have reserved.

Alumnae Memorandum Page

Alumnae Memorandum Page

Alumnae Memorandum Page

Helpful Words for the Alumnae Cookbook

From Members of the Alumnae.

A small drop of ink
Falling like dew upon a thought.—BYRON.

MISS VIRGINIA MAITLAND.

"Wishing you every success in your undertaking."

MISS GRACE E. SPIEGLE.

"I received the enclosed list from Miss Baldwin [names of possible contributors], and we both hope it will be of some use to you."

MISS CLARA J. HENDLEY.

"I think the cookbook idea a capital one, and I hope you will have no difficulty in finding contributors, and that the sale at the Bazar will be a great success."

MISS LINDA M. WHITAKER.

"I think the cookbook is a bright idea. Best wishes for the success of your plan."

Mrs. M. McCullough.

"I willingly will subscribe for the new cookbook, but have no recipe to contribute. Thanking you for your kindness in including me among the 100."

Miss Mary Kereven.

"If you will write to Mrs. ——, she will give you an excellent recipe. Mrs. —— makes a delicious fruit pie. I intended to send these recipes, but do not wish to keep you longer waiting for my answer."

Miss Mary S. Holmes.

"I do wish you success, for this sort of thing is no light matter."

Miss A. C. Voute.

"I delayed replying to your note in hopes of obtaining definite information for you. Should I have anything more satisfactory I will communicate with you. Hoping the information [given] may be of service to you."

Miss Sophie Schrader.

"These receipts were sent to me. I hope they are not too late for use."

Miss Louise H. Haeseler.

"I have not my list of addresses with me where I am spending the summer. I have forwarded your note to another member of our class, and no doubt she will attend to it."

Miss H. C. Leypoldt.

"Sends the above addresses, all of Philadelphia."

Miss Adah V. Hubbs.

"Enclosed you will find the names of those of my class whom I imagine are, or should be, best versed in matters pertaining to culinary art."

Miss Isabella M. Wilbur.

"May these messengers of good things find a warm welcome in many homes."

Misses E. L. Ridgely, Bessie H. Du Bois, Blanche Baldwin, C. M. Taylor, A. P. Wylie

kindly sent lists of possible contributors.

Alumnae Memorandum Page

Alumnae Memorandum Page

Alumnae Memorandum Page

INDEX.

	Page
NOTE OF THANKS	3
OVERHEARD	5
SOUPS, FISH AND SHELLFISH	7
SOUP, Black Bean	7
Calf's Head	8
Clam	7
FISH, Salmon, baked	9
Sheepshead, boiled	9
SHELLFISH, Clams, deviled	12
Lobster cutlets	13
Oysters, creamed	10
Oysters, croquettes	10
Oysters, fried	10
Oysters, pie	11
DISHES FOR BREAKFAST, LUNCHEON, OR TEA	17
Almonds, salted	23
Beans, Philadelphia baked	22
Beef, pressed	19
Birds without heads	18
Chicken salad	19
Chicken terrapin	18
Corn fritters	22
Cream dressing	23
Kidney, beef	17
Maccaroni, with cheese	20
Potato croquettes	21
Potato fricassee	21
Potato omelette	21
Tamales, Mexican	17
Tomatoes, baked	22
Tomatoes, salad	23
Welsh rarebit	20

	Page
PICKLES AND SAUCES	27
Catsup, cold, Mrs. P's	29
Catsup, cold, Mrs. R's	30
Cherries, pickled	28
Cucumber pickles	27
Currant Soy	27
Parker House Dressing	29
Peaches, pickled	28
Sauce, Chili	29
Sauce, Grandma Slifer's ketchup	31
Tomato ketchup	30
BREAD, ROLLS AND HOT CAKES	35
Bread, corn	36
Bread, homemade	35
Batter cakes	38
Biscuit, hot	37
Graham Gems	37
Muffins	38
Muffins, Milton	38
Pop overs	37
Sally Lunn	36
Yeast, homemade	35
PUDDINGS AND PASTRY	41
Custard, chocolate	45
Custard, French	45
Dessert, a palatable	44
Mince-meat, temperance	49
Mush, blackberry	41
Pudding, boiled fruit	43
Pudding, cabinet	46
Pudding, cherry	41
Pudding, Indian	43
Pudding, Maryland	42
Pudding, papa's	42
Pudding, plum	42
Pudding, excellent rice	44
Pudding, rice	44
Pudding, snow	45
Pie, cheese cake	47

	Page
Pie, cheese custard	48
Pie, mock mince-meat	48
Tart, hazlenut	47
ICES AND SWEETS	53
Frozen Charlotte Russe	54
Frozen custard	53
Frozen strawberries	53
French tapioca	55
Fruit candy	56
Fruit gelatine	54
Lemon butter, Mrs. L's	56
Lemon butter, Mrs. M's	56
Orange meringue	54
Taffy, Alumnæ	56
CAKES	61
Biscuit, sugar	61
Cakes, butter	63
Cakes, Scotch	63
Cakes, soft gingerbread	62
Cakes, York State snaps	64
Cake, almond cream	69
Cake, boiled sponge	68
Cake, delicate	68
Cake, Dutch	64
Cake, Edge Hill	70
Cake, fruit	66
Cake, Hartford Tea	65
Cake, Long Island	65
Cake, layer sponge	70
Cake, soft icing	67
Cake, spice	71
Cake, sponge	68
Cake, sponge ginger	69
Cake, Stock Grange	66
Cake, Washington	67
Cookies, Moravian Christmas	61
Doughnuts	62
Macaroons, shellbark	63
HELPFUL WORDS	75, 76, 77

www.ingramcontent.com/pod-product-compliance
Lightning Source LLC
Chambersburg PA
CBHW031606110426
42742CB00037B/1306